21ˢᵗ Century Junior Library

WORKING AT A HOSPITAL

by Pam Rosenberg

CHERRY LAKE PUBLISHING * ANN ARBOR, MICHIGAN

Published in the United States of America by Cherry Lake Publishing
Ann Arbor, Michigan
www.cherrylakepublishing.com

Content Adviser: Sharon Castle, PhD, Associate Professor of Elementary Social Studies, George Mason University, Fairfax, Virginia

Reading Consultant: Cecilia Minden-Cupp, PhD, Literacy Specialist and Author

Cover and page 4, ©iStockphoto.com/appleuzr; cover and page 6, ©iStockphoto.com/mayakova; cover and page 8, ©iStockphoto.com/jsmith; cover and page 10, TK; page 12, ©iStockphoto.com/leezsnow; page 14, ©Janine Wiedel Photolibrary/Alamy; page 16, ©Custom Medical Stock Photo/Alamy; page 18, ©Blend Images/Alamy; page 20, ©iStockphoto.com/pic trough

LIBRARY OF CONGRESS CATALOGING-IN-PUBLICATION DATA
Rosenberg, Pam.
  Working at a hospital / by Pam Rosenberg.
     p. cm.—(21st century junior library)
  Includes index.
  ISBN-13: 978-1-60279-264-7
  ISBN-10: 1-60279-264-X
  1. Hospitals—Employees—Juvenile literature. 2. Medical
personnel—Juvenile literature. I. Title. II. Series.
  RA972.5.R67 2009
  362.11—dc22   2008012207

Cherry Lake Publishing would like to acknowledge the work of
The Partnership for 21st Century Skills.
Please visit www.21stcenturyskills.org for more information.

CONTENTS

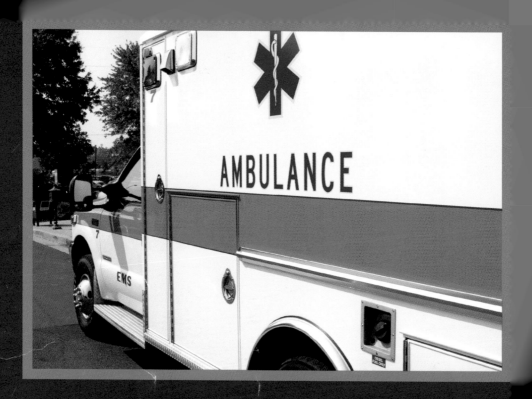

People who are very sick are taken to a hospital in an ambulance.

What Is a Hospital?

Do you hear a loud siren? It is an **ambulance**. It is racing down the street. Everyone needs to get out of the way! A person is very sick or hurt. The ambulance must get to the **hospital** fast!

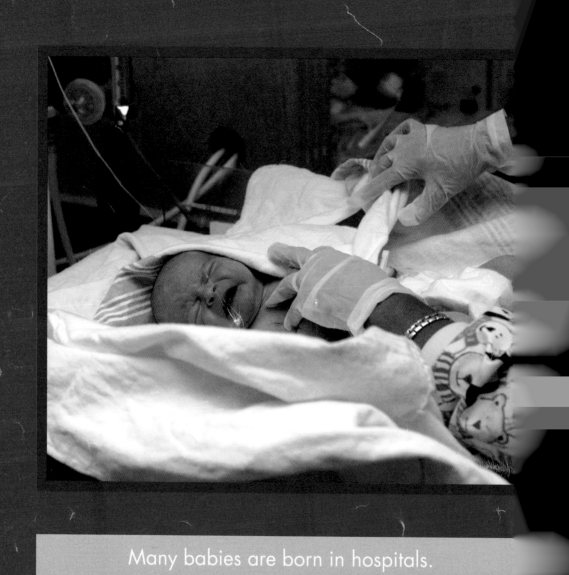

Many babies are born in hospitals.

People go to a hospital when they are sick or hurt. Doctors, nurses, and others help people get better.

Have you ever been to a hospital? Were you sick? Did you visit a friend? If you were at a hospital, you saw many people working there. Let's read about some hospital workers.

Think!

A lot of kids have been in a hospital. They just don't remember being there. Why don't they remember? Hint: Think about where most babies are born.

Babies don't remember being in the hospital. If this was your answer, then you are correct!

Doctors listen to your heart and lungs. The sounds they hear can help them figure out how to help you.

Hospital Workers

Many doctors work in their offices and in hospitals. Doctors help people find out why they are sick. Then they figure out how to help people get better. Your doctor will examine you if you feel sick. You might be sent to a hospital for some tests. People who are very sick stay at the hospital overnight.

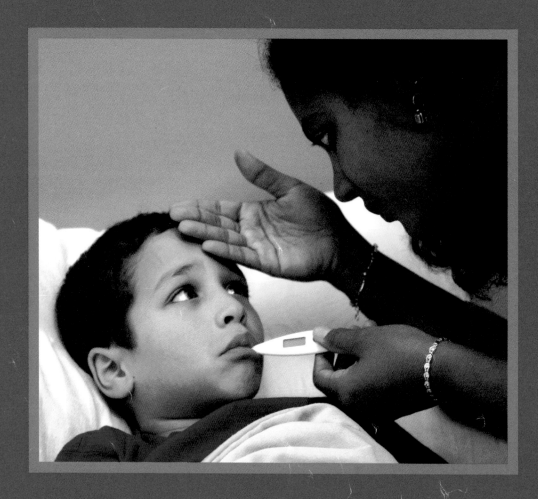

A nurse checks to see if a boy has a fever. Nurses do many things to to help patients feel better.

Nurses help take care of you at a hospital. They bring you **medicine**. They check to see if you have a **fever**. They watch you to see how you are doing. Nurses make sure that other hospital workers do their part to take care of you, too.

Some workers are trained to do special tests on your blood. Other workers take special pictures of your bones and organs. **X-rays** are one kind of special picture. Doctors use these pictures to see inside your body.

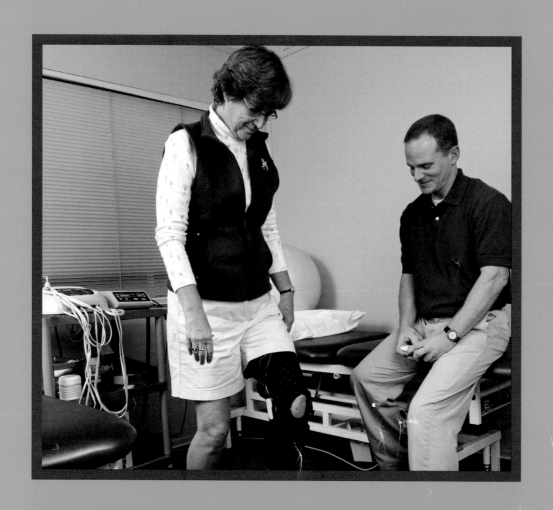

Physical therapists help people do
special exercises.

Physical therapists are people who help **patients** do special exercises. The exercises make them stronger. There are also other kinds of therapists. They help people with speaking, hearing, and other daily activities.

Create!

Draw a picture of one kind of hospital worker. Show the worker doing one part of the job. Be sure to show the tools needed to do the job.

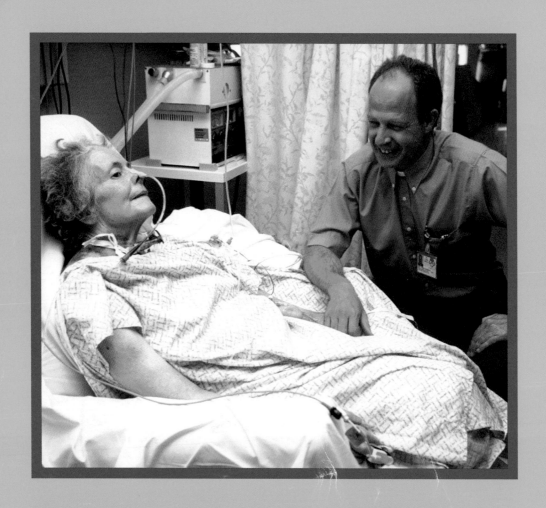

Chaplains visit patients in hospitals. They talk to patients and pray with them.

Being sick or hurt can be scary.
Chaplains help patients and their families.
They comfort them by listening. Chaplains
talk to people and pray with them.

There are some hospital workers that
patients hardly ever see. Some of them work
in the hospital kitchen. They help prepare
meals for patients and visitors.

Other workers help keep the hospital
clean. They wash floors and clean rooms.
It is important to keep the hospital clean and
germ free.

Some hospital workers do their jobs in an office.
Patients usually do not see them.

Some workers do their jobs in the hospital's offices. They take care of running the hospital. **Accountants** manage a hospital's money. **Lawyers** make sure the hospital follows all of its rules. Some people even have the job of hiring all of the other workers for the hospital!

Make a Guess!

Guess which three jobs most people think of when they think about hospital workers. Then ask five people to name three hospital jobs. Write down their answers. Add up the number of times each job was listed. Did the three jobs listed the most times match your guesses?

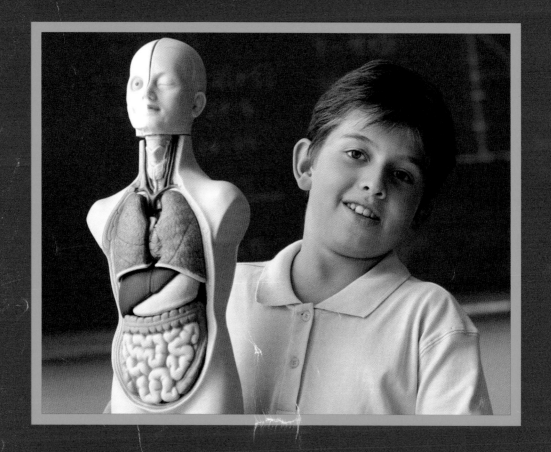

You need to learn about the human body to do
many hospital jobs.

Do You Want to Work at a Hospital?

What do you want to do when you grow up? Do you think you might like to work in a hospital? You can start getting ready now.

Start learning about the human body. Learn how it works. Find out what people can do to stay healthy.

Do you like to help prepare healthy meals at home? Maybe you would like to work in the kitchen at a hospital someday.

Most people who work in hospitals like to take care of people. You can practice at home. Help your parents keep your house clean. Help prepare meals. Learn about healthy eating.

A hospital can be a great place to work. Learn as much as you can now. It will help you decide if working at a hospital is right for you!

Ask Questions!

Do you know any adults who work in a hospital? If you do, ask them about their jobs. Find out what they had to study in school. Asking questions is a good way to learn about jobs that you are interested in.

GLOSSARY

accountants (uh-KOUN-tuhnts) people who are experts at managing money

ambulance (AM-bhuh-luhns) a vehicle that takes people who are sick or hurt to the hospital

chaplains (CHAP-luhnz) priests, ministers, rabbis, or other people who work in hospitals, lead prayers, and help comfort patients and their families

fever (FEE-vur) if your body is warmer than about 99 degrees Fahrenheit (37 degrees Celsius), you are too warm and have a fever

hospital (HOS-pih-tuhl) a place where people who are sick or hurt get help from doctors, nurses, and other workers

lawyers (LOI-urz) people who are trained to give advice about rules, or laws

medicine (MED-uh-suhn) a drug used to help sick people get better

patients (PAY-shuhnts) people who are being treated by doctors or other health care workers

physical therapists (FIZ-uh-kuhl THER-uh-pists) people who are trained to help treat muscles and joints that are damaged by sickness or injury

X-rays (EKS-rayz) pictures of bones and other organs inside the body that are taken with invisible high-energy light beams that can go through solid things

FIND OUT MORE

BOOKS

Aylmore, Angela. *We Work at the Hospital.* Chicago: Heinemann Library, 2006.

Kalman, Bobbie. *Hospital Workers in the Emergency Room.* New York: Crabtree Publishing Company, 2005.

Minden, Cecilia, and Linda M. Armantrout. *Nurses.* Chanhassen, MN: The Child's World, 2006.

WEB SITES

KidsHealth—Going to a Physical Therapist
www.kidshealth.org/kid/feel_ better/people/physical_therapy.html
Learn more about what a physical therapist does

KidsHealth—Going to the Hospital
www.kidshealth.org/kid/feel_ better/places/hospital.html
Read about what it is like when you have to stay in a hospital

INDEX

ABOUT THE AUTHOR

Pam Rosenberg is a former teacher who currently works as a writer and editor of children's books. She lives in Arlington Heights, Illinois.